The Teacher with the Allig

Miss Lucy had a student.
His name was Oliver Sneed.
She sat him at a table
to see if he could read.

Poetry

Counting Books

Science

Fairy Tales

3

He ate up all the crayons.
He drank up all the glue.
He tried to eat the pencils.

What did Miss Lucy do?

Miss Lucy called the principal.
Miss Lucy called the nurse.
Miss Lucy called the teacher with the alligator purse.

In came the principal.

In came the nurse.

In came the teacher with the alligator purse.

"I know!" said the teacher with the alligator purse.

11

"**Books!**" said the teacher with the alligator purse.

13

Out went the principal.
Out went the nurse.

Out went the teacher with the alligator purse.

Miss Lucy had a student.
His name was Oliver Sneed.

With **time,** and **love,** and lots of **books**
he learned how to read!